Table of Contents

Rourke
Educational Media
A Division of
Carson Dellosa Education
rourkeeducationalmedia.com

Can you find these words?

burrow

fruit

habitat

seeds

My Pet Hamster

A hamster is a great pet.

There are big hamsters.

There are small hamsters.

A hamster needs a **habitat**.
My hamster has a cage.

The cage has a wheel.

My hamster likes to dig.
It likes to **burrow**.

burrow

My hamster likes to run.

My hamster likes to eat.

I feed my hamster **seeds**.

seeds

11

I feed it **fruit**. I feed it vegetables.

fruit

I take care of my pet hamster.

Did you find these words?

It likes to **burrow**.

I feed it **fruit**.

A hamster needs a **habitat**.

I feed my hamster **seeds**.

Photo Glossary

 **burrow** (BUR-oh): To dig, live, or spend time in a hole made by an animal.

 **fruit** (froot): The fleshy, juicy part of a plant that contains seeds and is usually edible.

 **habitat** (HAB-i-tat): The place where an animal or plant lives.

 **seeds** (seeds): The parts of a flowering plant from which a new plant can grow.

Index

About the Author

Barry Cole lives in sunny Florida and enjoys living a healthy lifestyle along with his five-year-old son, Brody. His interests include jiu jitsu, running, boating, and anything outdoors.

© 2020 Rourke Educational Media

www.rourkeeducationalmedia.com

PHOTO CREDITS: Cover ©anopdesignstock; Pg 2, 11, 14,15 ©AngiePhotos; Pg 2, 12, 14, 15 ©RinoCdZ; Pg 2, 6-7, 14, 15 ©MartinLisner; Pg 2, 8, 14, 15 ©Kerrick; Pg 3 ©khilagan; Pg 4-5 ©gurinaleksandr; Pg 9 ©artisteer; Pg 10 ©wwspectrelabs

Edited by: Keli Sipperley
Cover design by: Rhea Magaro-Wallace
Interior design by: Kathy Walsh

Library of Congress PCN Data
Hamster / Barry Cole
(My Pet)
ISBN 978-1-73160-567-2 (hard cover)(alk. paper)
ISBN 978-1-73160-409-5 (soft cover)
ISBN 978-1-73160-616-7 (e-Book)
ISBN 978-1-73160-649-5 (ePub)
Library of Congress Control Number: 2018967362

Printed in the United States of America,
North Mankato, Minnesota